Peter Cameron

Notes on a collection of Hymenoptera from Greymouth, New Zealand, with descriptions of new species

Peter Cameron

Notes on a collection of Hymenoptera from Greymouth, New Zealand, with descriptions of new species

ISBN/EAN: 9783741130564

Manufactured in Europe, USA, Canada, Australia, Japa

Cover: Foto ©Thomas Meinert / pixelio.de

Manufactured and distributed by brebook publishing software
(www.brebook.com)

Peter Cameron

Notes on a collection of Hymenoptera from Greymouth, New Zealand, with descriptions of new species

Manchester Memoirs, Vol. xlii (1898), *No.* **1.**

i. Notes on a Collection of Hymenoptera from Greymouth, New Zealand, with descriptions of New Species.

By PETER CAMERON.

[*Communicated by J. Cosmo Melvill, M.A., F.L.S.*]

Received October 12th. Read October 19th, 1897.

The species of Hymenoptera enumerated and described in this paper were collected in the vicinity of Greymouth, New Zealand, by the late Mr. Richard Helms, whose assiduous labours have added so much to our knowledge of the Insect Fauna of New Zealand, and who, after his departure therefrom, did equally good work in investigating the Natural History of Australia.

Our earliest information on the Hymenoptera we owe to Fabricius, whose types are now in the Banksian Cabinet in the British Museum ; then, at a long interval, followed Francis Walker, who described some *Chalcididæ* collected by Darwin during the memorable voyage of the " Beagle," in his " Monographia Chalciditum," 1839 ; F. Smith, in his Catalogue of Hymenoptera in the British Museum ; and Mayr and Sichel in "Reise der Novara," 1867. Then in 1876 came F. Smith's important papers, " Descriptions of New Species of Hymenopterous Insects of New Zealand, collected by C. M. Wakefield, Esq., principally in the neighbourhood of Canterbury " (*Trans. Entom. Soc.* 1876, pp. 473-487) ; " Descriptions of Three New Species of Hymenoptera (*Formicidæ*) from New Zealand," *l.c.* pp. 489-

February 4th, 1898.

492 ; followed in the same *Transactions*, 1878, pp. 1-7, by
" Descriptions of New Species of Hymenopterous Insects
from New Zealand, collected by Prof. Hutton, at Otago."
Mr. W. F. Kirby (*Trans. Entom. Soc.* 1881, pp. 35-50) continued Mr. Smith's work with "A list of the Hymenoptera of New Zealand," and, *l.c.* 1883, pp. 199-202,
contributed " Notes on New or little-known Species of
Hymenoptera, chiefly from New Zealand."

In *Bull. Soc. Entom. Ital.*, xvi., 1884, Signor Gribodo
described *Agenia Brouni*; in *Trans. New Zealand Inst.*,
xvii., pp. 158 and 159, Mr. Colenso described *Rhyssa
clavula* and *Lissonota multicolor*; in *Manchester Memoirs*,
1887-8-9, I described five new species from Greymouth ;
in *Entom. Mon. Mag.*, iii (2), p. 275, the Rev. T. A. Marshall
described *Tanyzonus bolitophilæ* [= *Betyla fulva* Cam.]
which, with a *Diapria* described by Mr. Maskell (*Trans.
New Zealand Inst.*, xi., p. 230), the catalogue of Captain
Hutton, and the descriptions of *Hubertia*, &c., by Prof.
Forel in *C. R. Soc. Entom. Belg.*, 1890, completes our
narrative of the history of the literature of New Zealand
Hymenoptera.

Mr. Kirby in his list enumerated 81 species, from
which two may safely be deducted—one *Ophion luteus* Fab.,
a common European species recorded by Fabricius, doubt-
less in error, one of the native species having been
probably mistaken for it ; and *Blennocampa adumbrata*
Klug, the common European slug-worm, described by Mr.
Kirby as *Monostegia antipoda.* This leaves 79 as the
total number known as inhabitants of the islands in 1881 ;
add thereto five (one species, *Priocnemis Pascoei* Kirby,
was described in error) recorded in Kirby's paper of 1883,
Gribodo's *Agenia Brouni*, Colenso's *Rhyssa* and *Lissonota*,
my three specimens described in 1888, the two in 1889,
and the 34 new species now described give us a total of
121 species known from New Zealand.

This undoubtedly marks a gratifying increase of knowledge since 1881 ; but I am certain that, if the islands were to be again explored by a naturalist of the calibre of Mr. Helms, the list might easily be doubled, particularly if unworked localities were investigated.

It is more than probable that many of the species are very local in their distribution, as is the case with Lepidoptera and Coleoptera. On this point the following remarks of Mr. E. Meyrick *(Proc. Entom. Soc.* 1883, p. 29) throw some light on the peculiarities of the New Zealand Insect Fauna. " The islands were composed partly of bare mountain ranges, partly of low-lying forest. The mountains, although very bleak and shelterless, had an extensive and varied fauna, fresh species of insects occurring on every mountain visited ; the genus *Crambus*, for example, was represented by a variety of species, for which there seemed to be no special reason. On the other hand, the forests, which comprised a remarkable number of trees and shrubs apparently well suited for food, were strangely deficient in insects, and further, the same species occurred nearly throughout the islands. It appeared, in fact, that a vast number of situations suitable for insects was not utilised. This was the case with the Lepidoptera and Coleoptera and probably with other insects." The parasitic species are probably not very numerous, their places being taken by the parasitic Diptera. At present the Diptera slightly exceed the Hymenoptera in number of species.

As regards the affinities of the New Zealand species the relationship to Australia is not very great. It is indicated on the one hand by the presence of the Australian genera *Lamprocolletes, Dasycolletes, Leioproctus* and *Rhagigaster ;* and by species common alike to the Islands and to Australia or Tasmania. These species are *Leioproctus imitatus* Sm. found in Australia, *Lamprocolletes*

obscurus Sm. in Tasmania, *Prosopis vicina* Sichel in
Tasmania, and the Ichneumon "*Rhyssa*" *semipuncta*
Kirby, which seems to be a common Australian species.
Of the Aculeates, the Bees and *Pompilidæ* are the
most numerous in species. The latter appear to be,
judging from the collecting of Mr. Helms, the most
numerous in individuals, as they are the most striking in
size, form, and coloration. Their great abundance would
seem to indicate a rich and varied arachnid Fauna ; for
the *Pompilidæ* store their nests with spiders. Next to
the *Pompilidæ*, the family most numerous in species is
the *Larridæ*, which prey on *Orthoptera*. Among the
parasitic forms the genus *Ichneumon* possesses the greatest
number of species, some of which are very large and
handsome creatures.

Although, of course, there can be no genetic relationship between the Hymenopterous Fauna of New Zealand
and the Hawaiian Islands, yet a comparison between the
two brings out some very interesting features. *Pison* is
not a large genus, but it is very widely spread over the
globe. It is not uncommon in Australia, is represented
in the Malay Archipelago, by one species in Tahiti, and by
two in Hawaii. *Prosopis*, a bee genus, has twelve species
in Hawaii, as against seven in New Zealand, it is common
in Australia and is of almost world-wide distribution.
The *Larridæ* are fairly well represented in New Zealand,
but are quite absent from Hawaii. The *Crabronidæ* again
are much more numerous in the last mentioned locality—
ten species as against four in New Zealand, the two latter
belonging to a group (*Rhopalum*) not found in Hawaii
at all. It is, however, in the dominant group in each of the
localities where we find the most remarkable distinction.
The characteristic family in New Zealand is the *Pompilidæ*, in Hawaii the *Vespidæ*, neither being represented
in the other islands ; both families, moreover, being common

in Australia and Tasmania—why this should be so it is difficult to understand. The absence of *Pompilidæ* in Hawaii may be owing to the scarcity of spiders there : but on this point I have no information. The absence of the *Odyneridæ* in New Zealand cannot be owing to the absence there of their food, for it is as common as, if not more abundant than, it is in the Sandwich Islands. The absence of *Tachytes*, &c., in the Hawaii Islands may be caused by there being no crickets living there.

The paucity of *Formicidæ* in species is remarkable. All the species are endemic, two of the genera being peculiar. I cannot, however, understand how, while in the Sandwich Islands there are at least five ants of almost world-wide distribution, *e.g.*, *Ponera contracta*, *Prenolepis longicornis*, *Tetramorium guineense*, none of them should have been recorded from New Zealand, where one would think the environment is eminently suitable and the commercial intercourse with other regions even more extensive.

As respects the species added by Mr. Helms to the Fauna, the most noteworthy are those belonging to the genera *Dicoelotus*, *Hemiteles*, *Chorinæus*, *Bassus*, *Ascogaster*, *Meteorus*, and *Alysia*, those genera not having been previously recorded. Of the species, *Ichneumon hersilia*, which differs markedly from the others in structure, is perhaps the most interesting.

TENTHREDINIDÆ.

No native species of this family is known ; but the common European slug-worm of the pear (*Blennocampa adumbrata*) has been introduced, and recorded by Captain Hutton in his list as *Blennocampa cerasi ;* by Mr. F. Smith (*Trans. Entom. Soc.*, 1876, p. 474) as *Blennocampa adumbrata* Klug ; and it has been described by Mr. W. F. Kirby (*Trans. Entom. Soc.*, 1881, p. 50) as a new species under the name of *Monostegia antipoda. Monostegia* is not a valid genus, being founded on a character which is not constant even in the same species. Thus *Eriocampa adumbrata* is frequently found with only one median cellule in the hind wings, instead of the normal two. Mr. Helms sends it from Greymouth.

SIRICIDÆ.

XIPHIDRIA DECEPTA.

Derecyrta deceptus Sm., *Trans. Entom. Soc.*, 1876, p. 474, pl. 4, f. 6.

Xiphidria flavopicta Sm., *l.c.* 1878, p. 1.

As figured by Smith this species is shown of a much too uniform colour ; the eye orbits, the lines on vertex, the face and edge of the pronotum are clear pale yellow ; the mesonotum dark ferruginous, suffused with black ; the basal four segments of the abdomen clear reddish, and the legs bright pale yellow. On the other hand, the thorax above frequently wants the yellow marks found in the type, the scutella, for example, not being differently coloured from the mesonotum, while again the wings are clear, not fulvo-hyaline. I suspect, however, that my three examples are immature, a circumstance which makes wood-feeding insects have the markings and colour less distinct ; although it must be said that the yellow on the head and the rufous colour on the abdomen are bright enough in my two males, the ♀ being coloured more as in Smith's figure.

ICHNEUMONIDÆ.

ICHNEUMON.

A. Scutellum largely elevated, oblique, its top depressed in the middle, the sides rounded ; the tubercles largely projecting, much larger than usual, somewhat triangular, but with the apex rounded ; the median segment not tuberculate nor spined.

ICHNEUMON HERSILIA, *sp. nov.*

*Rufus, thorace nigro et albo-maculato ; pedibus rufis ;
alis fulvo-hyalinis, stigmate nigro.* ♂. Long. 11 mm.

Head rufous ; the inner orbits narrowly below, broadly
above, and the sides of the clypeus, yellow ; the ocellar
region, the front, and the occiput, black ; the vertex bare ;
the face covered with short fuscous hair ; the mandibles
rufous, the teeth black ; the face roundly projecting in the
middle, strongly but not closely punctured ; the hollowed
front finely transversely striated ; the palpi rufous. Prothorax black, broadly rufous above ; the mesonotum has
the sides and base, broadly in the middle, black ; the rest
rufous, with a large yellow mark at the apex. The scutellum yellow, a rufous splash at the base ; its height is
nearly equal to its width at the bottom ; the basal keels
are curved and reach to the middle ; the top is irregularly
divided, one lobe being wider than the other. The
median segment is gradually rounded to the apex ; the
areæ distinct ; the supramedian widely separated from
the base of the segment, longer than broad, a little
narrowed towards the base, which is rounded ; the
sides straight ; the posterior median black, transversely
striated ; the other areæ smooth and shining ; the
base of the segments broadly black ; the sides are
also edged with black ; and, in front of the coxæ,
there is a large yellow mark touching the keel.   The
propleuræ broadly black in the middle ; the mesopleuræ at and including the tubercles white, the lower
part rufous, with a large white mark in the centre, and
the sternum is rufous ; there is a broad black oblique band
in the middle ; and the apex is black, narrowly so on the
lower side ; the breast black in front. Legs entirely
rufous, as is also the abdomen.   The stigma and nervures
black ; the areolet almost triangular, the nervures being

narrowed at the top, where it is in width less than the space bounded by the recurrent and the second transverse cubital nervures ; the transverse median nervure is interstitial. Abdomen smooth, shining, impunctate ; the gastrocœli are indicated by a shallow depression.

The scutellum in this species might refer it to *Hoplismenus,* but it differs from that in having no spines on the median segment. The shape of the scutellum is quite similar to what it is in some Mexican species of *Ichneumon, e.g. I. aztecus.*

B. Scutellum flat, normal.

ICHNEUMON ACTISTA, *sp. nov.*

Niger, thorace coxisque albo-maculatis ; pedibus rufis ; alis fere hyalinis, stigmate nervisque nigris, ♂. Long. 14 mm.

Antennæ black ; the scape with a yellow mark in the middle on the lower side. Head : the face below the antennæ, the mandibles except the teeth, the palpi, a mark on the vertex touching the eyes, and a larger mark behind lower down, yellow ; almost impunctate, the front and vertex thickly covered with short blackish hair, the labrum fringed with longish fulvous hair ; behind, it is as long as the eyes and sharply oblique. Thorax oblique in front ; the sides of the pronotum widely, a large square mark on the mesonotum in the middle, the scutellum, postscutellum, the supramedian area of the metanotum, two large marks on the mesopleuræ, the anterior slightly the larger, and a large oblique mark on the metapleuræ, yellow. Metanotal areæ well developed ; the keels acute, the supramedian rounded at the base ; the sides straight, gradually narrowed to the apex, which is transverse ; the apex has an oblique slope. The four anterior coxæ are white beneath ; the hinder have a large white mark at the base above and beneath ; the trochanters are black. The alar nervures and stigma are deep black ; the transverse basal nervure is interstitial ; the areolet is narrowed at the top, being there in length less than the space bounded by the recurrent and the second transverse cubital nervures. Abdomen deep black, very smooth, shining ; the gastrocœli shallow, smooth, indistinct.

ICHNEUMON HELMSII, sp. nov.

Niger, abdomine pedibusque rufis ; scutello flavo ; alis fulvo-hyalinis, stigmate fulvo. ♂. Long. 15 mm.

Antennæ black ; the scape with a yellow mark in the middle beneath ; the apical joints dilated on the lower side, the scape thickly covered with longish black hair. Face with clypeus strongly punctured, thickly covered with short white hair ; the sides of the clypeus, a broad mark on the cheeks close to the eyes, with its top obliquely truncated and narrow, projecting obliquely from the base of the truncated part into a pear-shaped mark, which extends in the middle beyond the base of the antennae, but not uniting there, the labrum and palpi, yellow ; the tips of the mandibles piceous ; their basal half strongly punctured. Behind the eyes the head is obliquely narrowed ; the hinder part rather deeply and roundly narrowed inwardly and margined ; mesonotum and upper part of the pronotum closely and strongly punctured ; the lower part of the propleuræ smooth and shining ; the prosternum closely punctured. Scutellum entirely yellow, smooth, shining, flat ; the postscutellum punctured. Median segment coarsely and irregularly punctured ; the supramedian area almost square, but slightly narrowed towards the apex ; the base and apex transverse ; the apex of the segment with an oblique slope ; coarsely, irregularly, transversely striolated and reticulated ; its centre deeply furrowed at the base ; the keels bordering it distinct, curved ; the lateral keels

on the top stout, ending in the middle in a stout, flat, triangular tooth. Meso- and meta-pleuræ strongly punctured,
the latter on the lower side with a curved keel. The coxæ
and base of the trochanters are black ; the hinder coxæ
have a reddish mark on the apex behind ; the extreme apex
of the hinder femora black ; the apices of the hinder tibiæ
and of the tarsal joints infuscated. The wing nervures to
the stigma, and the stigma itself, fulvous, the apical
nervures black ; the areolet narrowed at the top, being
there distinctly less in length than the space bounded by
the recurrent and the second transverse cubital nervures.
The apex of the petiole closely, longitudinally striated,
and marked with yellow at the sides ; down the sides
from the base is a narrow black line which is continued
down the middle to opposite the spiracles, becoming
thickened towards the apex ; the spiracles are bordered
with black ; the other segments are closely punctured ;
the second and third have the sides at the apex yellowish ;
the gastrocœli deep, wide at the apex, being somewhat
triangular seen from the outer side ; smooth, shining, the
middle at the apex with a few striæ.

This is the largest and stoutest-looking species of the
New Zealand species of *Ichneumon*, and is very distinct
from any of them.

ICHNEUMON DECEPTUS Sm.

Smith (*Trans. Entom. Soc.*, 1876, p. 477) only describes
the ♀ of this species, so I now describe the ♂.

Scape of the antennæ beneath, the face below the
antennæ, the mandibles except the teeth, the palpi, a
broad line on the outer orbits of the eyes on the lower
side, the pronotum broadly, a squarish mark in the centre
of the mesonotum, the scutellum, post-scutellum, a square
mark on the median segment, a mark on the base of the
mesopleuræ, a smaller one at the apex lower down, a

small one on the apex of the propleuræ and a large one at
the apex of the metapleuræ, yellow ; the four anterior
coxæ are yellow as are also the trochanters, the rest of the
legs having also a yellowish hue ; the hinder coxæ and
trochanters are black, the former with a large yellow mark
behind.   On the abdomen above, the fifth and sixth
segments are more or less black.   The wings vary in tint.

ICHNEUMON LOTATORIUS Fab.

Ichneumon lotatorius Fab. has been described by
Mr. W. F. Kirby (*Trans. Entom. Soc.*, 1883, p. 200) as an
aculeate under the name of *Priocnemis Pascoei.*   I have
examined the type in the British Museum.   It agrees
with *Ichneumon insidiator* Sm., and differs from the other
species in having the petiole black ; but *I. insidiator* has the
extreme apex of it yellowish, while *I. lotatorius* differs
from it in having the apex of the hinder femora and of
the hinder tibiæ black ; the mesonotum not distinctly
punctured, and only the second abdominal segment is
red, while in *I. insidiator* the second and third are entirely
yellow.

Smith (*Trans. Entom. Soc.*, 1876, p. 476) remarks that
his *I. insidiator* is probably the ♂ of *I. lotatorius*
Fab., but Mr. Kirby treats it as distinct.

As *I. lotatorius* has not been properly described I give
a description of both sexes here.

♂ Black ; the scutellum and tubercles yellow ; the
legs and second abdominal segment reddish-fulvous, the
front legs with a more yellowish tinge ; the coxæ, anterior
trochanters, the base of the posterior, the apex of the
hinder femora broadly, and the apex of the hinder tibiæ
more narrowly, black ; the wings fulvous or more or less
deeply smoky ; the stigma testaceous.

♀ Antennæ short, thick, involute; pruinose towards the
apex, the base with short black hair.   Head strongly

punctured, much more closely in the centre below the antennæ ; the oral region with the punctures much more widely separated and covered with longish fulvous hair ; the palpi testaceous ; the eyes margined distinctly. Pronotum closely punctured ; the mesonotum with the punctures more widely separated ; the scutellum almost impunctate ; median segment closely punctured ; the areæ all distinctly defined ; the supramedian longer than broad ; the apex is closely and somewhat coarsely transversely striated. Meso- and meta-pleuræ closely and strongly punctured. Coxæ strongly punctured. Abdomen smooth and shining, impunctate ; the gastrocœli impunctate. The areolet at the top narrowed, being there a little less than the space bounded by the recurrent and the second transverse cubital nervures ; the recurrent nervure is bent towards the apex of the wing near the middle, and has there a minute branch.

ICHNEUMON INSIDIATOR Sm.

Smith's description, which only relates to coloration, may be supplemented as regards other points.

Comparing it with the ♂ of *I. sollicitorius*, it may be known from it by the petiole being black, only yellow at the apex, whereas in *I. sollicitorius* it is entirely yellow ; the face is black in the middle, the thorax above and at the sides is much more strongly punctured, as are also the the coxæ ; the thorax is broader in front at the tegulæ ; the post-scutellum black ; the median segment strongly aciculated ; the transverse cubital nervure at the base in the middle, is angled with a short branch issuing backwards from the middle of the angle, whereas in *I. sollicitorius* it is rounded ; and the stigma is testaceous, not blackish.

ICHNEUMON SOLLICITORIUS Fab.

Apparently a common species. I have only seen the male.

ICHNEUMON ARTAXIDIA, *sp. nov.*

Capite thoraceque ferrugineis ; scutello flavo, abdomine nigro, basi late rufo-flavo ; pedibus rufo-fulvis, coxis trochanteribusque nigris; alis cum nervis flavis. ♂ . Long. 8 mm.

Scape of antennae dark-rufous, blackish above ; the flagellum absent. Head closely, but not strongly punctured ; covered rather closely with pale hair ; the clypeus with the hair longer and paler, and only with a few scattered punctures ; the labrum fringed with longer hair ; the mandibles strongly punctured ; their teeth black Thorax dark-ferruginous ; the prosternum, a large oblique. mark on the propleuræ, a large oblique mark on the mesopleuræ extending from the base to the apex, a mark on either side of the mesosternum at the apex, the metapleurae except the apex above and the sides of the median segment, black. Mesonotum closely punctured ; the scutellum, post-scutellum and the centre of the median segment at the base, yellow. The pro- and meso-pleuræ closely punctured ; the propleuræ with a few distinct striæ at the apex in the middle ; the top of the mesopleuræ at the apex and the metapleuræ smooth and shining ; the base of the metapleuræ with a wide, deep, crenulated furrow at the base. The median segment has no areæ, and the only keel is one bordering the apex above ; the sides at the apex between this keel and the lateral at the apex is irregularly crenulated. Abdomen smooth and shining ; the third and following segments black ; the gastrocœli indistinct.

ICHNEUMON IXIA, *sp. nov.*

Rufus, abdominis apice late nigro, scutello flavo ; alis hyalinis, stigmate flavo, nervis fuscis. ♀. Long. 7·5 mm.

Antennæ stout, involute, bare, obscure-rufous, the

flagellum darker above ; the scape with a few punctures on the under side.   Head dark-rufous ; the front and two large marks on the sides above the clypeus, black ; the vertex strongly punctured ; the face and clypeus with the punctures much fewer and more widely separated ; the face in the middle with a few fine transverse striations ; the front largely excavated, smooth and shining. The eyes distinctly margined ; the inner orbits narrowly lined with yellow. Mesonotum rufous, a broad black band down the centre and a narrower one down the sides ; closely, but not strongly, punctured. Scutellum rufous, the apex broadly yellow ; the apex almost impunctate ; the remainder bearing clearly separated, moderately large, punctures ; the post-scutellum for the greater part yellow. At the base of the scutellum is a wide, deep curved furrow. The median segment has a gradually rounded slope to the apex, which is oblique ; it is smooth and shining, almost bare ; the supramedian area is large, somewhat wider than long, rounded at the base, the sides straight, oblique ; the apex rounded on its inside ; the supra-external areæ are finely punctured ; the posterior median area is roundly excavated, not much narrowed towards the apex, and finely and closely punctured ; the posterior intermedian areæ are not so closely, but much more strongly, punctured ; and, at the top, is a yellowish mark ; the pro- and meso-pleuræ are strongly punctured, the former obscurely striated at the apex ; the mesopleuræ black, except a large rufous mark in the middle at the base and a larger one lower down at the apex ; the sternum for the most part black ; the metapleuræ very smooth, shining, impunctate, black, except over the coxæ. Legs dark rufous ; the anterior brighter in tint ; the hinder femora much darker, abdomen smooth and shining, the three basal segments red ; the apical black.

ICHNEUMON COLENSII, *sp. nov.*

Rufus ; orbitis oculorum, linea pronoti, lineis 2 mesonoti, scutello, post-scutelloque flavis ; abdominis apice late nigro ; alis fulvo-hyalinis, stigmate flavo. ♀. Long. 7 mm.

Scape of the antennæ dark-ferruginous, finely punctured, thickly covered with short dark hair, the flagellum black, paler on the lower side. Head rufous ; the vertex in the centre darker ; the inner orbits, broad at the top, narrow at the bottom, a curved line at the top, and the outer side beneath, lemon-yellow ; the face and vertex punctured, but not strongly, their sides almost impunctate ; the clypeus with a few scattered punctures ; the mandibles punctured, suffused with yellow at the base ; the apex black ; the palpi pale-yellow. Thorax rufous ; a broad line on the pronotum, the scutellum, post-scutellum, the lower side of the propleuræ and of the mesopleuræ broadly, two narrow lines on the centre of the mesonotum and the apex of the metapleuræ below, lemon-yellow. The mesonotum is punctured ; there is a central and two large lateral black marks, the latter bordered on the inner side by the yellow lines ; the apex of the scutellum is rufous, and it has a few shallow punctures. The median segment has an almost gradually rounded slope and is strongly punctured at the sides ; the areæ complete, the supramedian longer than broad, rounded at the base ; the pro- and meso-pleuræ closely punctured ; the propleuræ broadly black in the middle ; the mesopleuræ broadly black above and at the apex ; the metapleuræ very smooth and shining, impunctate. Legs uniformly rufous ; the fore coxæ pale-yellow ; there is a lemon-yellow mark over the hinder pair above at the base. Alar nervures dark fuscous, the stigma pale testaceous ; the areolet narrowed at the top. Abdomen smooth and shining ; the apical three segments black ; the gastrocœli indistinct, finely and closely punctured.

ICHNEUMON URSULA, *sp. nov.*

Ferrugineus, thorace nigro-maculato ; orbitis oculorum, linea pronoti, lineis 2 mesonoti scutelloque flavis ; alis fulvis stigmate nervisque fulvis. ♀. Long. 9 mm.

Head : the inner orbits to the hinder edge of the eyes above and a mark, longer than broad, on the outer edge beneath, yellow ; the vertex with shallow, widely separated punctures ; the front shining, impunctate, the middle with a few transverse striations ; the mandibles and palpi pallid-yellow ; the apex of the mandibles black ; the clypeus is very shining, with a few widely separated punctures. Antennæ broken off. Thorax : the edge of the pronotum, a line on the lower edge of the propleuræ, two lines in the middle of the mesonotum, the scutellum, post-scutellum, a mark over, and in front of, the middle and a smaller one over the hinder coxæ, lemon-yellow ; a mark at the base of the mesonotum in the centre, its apex being triangular, two broad lines down its sides outside the yellow ones and the scutellum and post-scutellum, lemon-yellow. The scutellum is broader than long, smooth, impunctate, the depression at its base black. The median segment strongly shagreened, more strongly on the sides at the apex ; the areæ complete ; the supramedian bluntly rounded at the base, the sides straight, a little narrowed towards the apex ; the posterior median of nearly equal width, not much hollowed in the centre, its apex with a few transverse striæ, the middle almost smooth, hardly shagreened. In the centre of the propleuræ is a large, somewhat triangular mark ; the mesopleuræ under the wings broadly, the mesosternum and the basal three-fourths of the metapleuræ, black. Legs uniformly ferruginous. Wings hyaline, but with a decided fulvous tinge ; the stigma narrowed at the top, being there narrower than the space bounded by the recurrent and the second transverse cubital nervures ; the latter is received shortly beyond the middle of the areolet. Abdomen smooth, shining, impunctate ; the fifth and sixth segments broadly black ; the gastrocœli shallow, not very distinct, finely aciculated. The ventral segments are pallid-yellow in the middle.

ICHNEUMON BROUNI, *sp. nov.*

Long. 7 mm. ♂.

A very similar species to *I. falsus*, but is smaller ; the sternum is black ; the hinder coxæ are without any black ; the petiole is smooth, not shagreened ; the gastrocœli are deeper and more clearly defined ; and the recurrent nervure is broadly curved, while in *I. falsus* it is slightly angled in the middle and emits there a short branch.

Antennæ black, the scape yellow beneath ; the apical joints of the flagellum dilated on lower side. Head pale-yellow ; the occiput, and the vertex and front broadly in the centre, black ; the tips of the mandibles black ; the face sparsely pilose ; the clypeus with longish pale, the vertex thickly covered with black hair ; shagreened ; the hollowed front smooth and shining. Thorax black ; a broad line of equal width on the pronotum, two lines on the mesonotum, scutellum, post-scutellum, the median segment, the lower edge of the pronotum, a short line opposite the tegulæ, the scutellar keels at the base, the scutellum, post-scutellum, two large marks on the apex of the median segment, the tubercles, the lower half of the mesopleuræ, and a line on the lower side of the propleuræ, lemon-yellow. The mesonotum has the punctures somewhat close together, those on the scutellum are larger and more widely separated ; the median segment has only a few minute punctures at the base. The propleuræ have the punctures shallow and widely separated ; the mesopleuræ are more strongly and closely punctured, except the usual smooth spot on the apex ; the metapleuræ smooth, impunctate. The base of the median segment, the supra and the posterior median areæ are blood-coloured ; the supramedian is not much wider than long. The median segment has a gradually rounded slope ; at the base of the median segment below the wings is a yellow and rufous spot. The areolet is triangular at the top, the nervures being almost united there. The four anterior coxæ, trochanters and lower side of the femora are lemon-yellow ; the rest fulvous; the hinder legs dark rufous, the tarsi paler ; the hinder coxæ black above, and to near the middle, the rest of the sides and their lower side fulvous ; at their base is a large, somewhat triangular lemon-yellow mark. The petiole is, towards the apex, roughly irregularly shagreened ; the other segments are closely punctured ; the gastrocœli shallow, at the base closely longitudinally striated.

ICHNEUMON FALSUS, *sp. nov.*

Niger ; ore, sterno, linea pronoti, scutello, lineis 2 mesonoti metanotoque flavis ; abdomine ferrugineo, apice late nigro ; pedibus anterioribus rufis, coxis trochanteribus que flavis, pedibus posticis fusco-ferrugineis ; alis fere hyalinis, stigmate nigro. ♂. Long. 10 mm.

Antennæ black, slightly brownish beneath ; the scape lemon-yellow on the under side. The face from below the antennæ, including the oral region, the mandibles and the palpi, the inner orbits narrowly to shortly below the ocelli, and the lower orbits—broadly beneath, narrowly above—lemon-yellow. The face strongly punctured, the clypeus with a few scattered punctures ; the frontal depression deep, shining, the edges aciculated. The line on the pronotum is broad and dilated at the base ; the two lines on the pronotum are also dilated at the base and extend to near the scutellum ; a mark on the lower half of the mesopleuræ and the sternum, lemon-yellow. The propleuræ impunctate ; the upper parts of the mesopleuræ at the base strongly punctured, the apical impunctate in the middle, and the metapleurae impunctate. The base of the median segment reddish (perhaps through discoloration) : the supramedian area a little broader than long, rounded at the base ; the posterior median complete ; the others obsolete. The alar stigma and nervures black ; the areolet at the top a little less in width than the space bounded by the recurrent and the second transverse cubital nervures. Legs fulvous ; the four anterior coxæ and trochanters lemon-yellow ; the hinder coxae fulvous like the femora and yellow at the base above and in the middle, the rest of them black. Abdomen reddish ; the apical three segments black above ; the base of the second segments shagreened ; the gastrocœli moderately wide, deep.

ICHNEUMON LEODACUS, *sp. nov.*

Ferrugineus, scutello flavo ; metapleuris, coxis trochanteribusque posticis nigris, alis flavis. ♂. Long. 8 mm.

Scape of antennæ rufous, punctured, thickly covered with pale hair ; the flagellum fuscous. Head : the face strongly punctured ; the clypeus shining, impunctate ; the face covered closely with short white hair ; the clypeus has the hair longer, sparser and darker in colour ; the vertex and occiput more closely punctured than the face ; the tips of mandibles black ; the palpi pale-testaceous ; the inner and outer orbits above reddish-yellow. Mesonotum shining, the sides finely and closely punctured, the middle almost impunctate. Scutellum and post-scutellum shining, impunctate, orange-yellow. The base of the

median segment rounded, the rest of it sharply oblique ;
the sides at the base shagreened ; the apex in the middle
transversely striated ; the rest coarsely shagreened. There
are no areæ, and only a stout curved keel over the oblique
keel. The propleuræ impunctate ; in the centre is a large
somewhat triangular black mark ; the mesopleuræ slightly
punctured ; in the centre at the apex is a black mark,
narrowed towards the apex ; immediately in front of the
middle coxæ is a larger, somewhat similarly shaped, black
mark ; the metapleuræ smooth, impunctate, black, except
an elongate mark at the top, and a shorter, broader and
more irregularly-shaped one over the coxæ. The legs
are uniformly coloured, except the hind coxæ and the
basal joint of the hinder trochanters, which are black. The
areolet is narrowed at the top, being there a little less than
the space bounded by the transverse cubital and the
recurrent nervures, the latter being received almost in the
centre of the cellule. Abdomen smooth, shining, impunctate ; the gastrocœli indistinct, closely punctured.

ICHNEUMON MACHIMIA, *sp. nov.*

*Niger, orbitis oculorum, linea pronoti, tegulisque scutelli
flavis ; abdomine rufo ; pedibus anticis rufis ; tibiis tarsisque
posterioribus sordide rufis ; alis fusco-hyalinis, stigmate
rufo-testaceo.* ♀. Long. 8 mm.

Front strongly punctured ; the clypeus shining and
bearing a few scattered punctures ; the vertex shagreened,
the ocellar region rough, the inner orbits and round the
top to opposite the tegulæ, as well as a line at the foot,
yellow ; the clypeus and labrum rufous (perhaps a dis-
coloured yellow) ; the mandibles a dirty yellow, the teeth
black ; the palpi yellow ; the face and clypeus have a few
white hairs. Antennæ black, the scape shining, and
bearing a few punctures. Thorax shining, the mesonotum
impunctate ; the median segment coarsely aciculated

The edge of the pronotum, tegulæ, two longitudinal lines on the mesonotum, the scutellum and post-scutellum, yellow. Median segment thickly covered with longish pale hair, coarsely aciculated, the areæ distinct except the posterior median, the keels of which are obliterated. The propleuræ, except at the base, closely obliquely striated, the striæ coarser on the lower side, the mesopleuræ rather strongly and distinctly punctured, the base of the median segment punctured, the rest longitudinally shagreened, running into striations on the lower side. All the coxæ and trochanters are black ; the fore femora, tibiæ and tarsi rufous, as are also the four posterior, but these are darker in tint, this being especially the case with the femora. Abdomen shining ; the apex of petiole closely punctured, the gastrocœli shallow, indistinct ; the sheaths of the ovipositor black.

Has the look and form of a *Cryptus*, but is a true *Ichneumon*.

ICHNEUMON UTETES, *sp. nov.*

Rufus, pleuris nigris ; femoribus posticis fuscis ; alis hyalinis, stigmate flavo, nervis fuscis. ♀. Long. 5 mm.

Antennæ short, stout, almost bare, if anything thickened beyond the middle, uniformly rufous. Head rufous, the vertex darker, the excavated front black ; the face strongly punctured ; the clypeus with only a few shallow punctures ; the front transversely striated in the middle ; the vertex and occiput closely and rather strongly punctured ; the outer orbits, except at the top, very smooth, and shining, and with only a few shallow scattered punctures ; the mandibles rufous, their teeth black ; the palpi testaceous. Thorax rufous ; the mesonotum in front infuscated ; the propleuræ black, except above and beneath ; the base indistinctly striated ; the mesopleuræ black, except a pale testaceous mark on the apex above the middle coxæ, the extreme base being rufous ; closely punctured ; the apex over the coxæ indistinctly and irregularly striolated ; the metapleuræ above very smooth and shining ; the lower part finely longitudinally striolated. The scutellum is, if anything, more strongly punctured than the mesonotum. The median segment has the areæ complete ; the supramedian area is transverse at the apex ; the top obliquely narrowed, the middle itself being transverse ; the apex of the segment has an oblique slope ; the middle is slightly hollowed, closely punctured ; the top almost smooth, the bottom obscurely transversely striated ; the posterior median area with straight sides ; the legs rufous ; the base of the middle coxæ and the hinder coxæ above, black ; the latter strongly punctured. Abdomen rufo-ferruginous, smooth and shining, glabrous except for a few hairs on the apex and sides ; the sides of the 2-5 segments blackish. The alar areolet narrowed at the top, being there in width very little less than the space bounded by the second transverse cubital and the recurrent nervures.

ICHNEUMON THYELLMA, *sp. nov.*

Long. 5·5 mm.

Comes near to *I. utetes*, with which it has a close resemblance in coloration, but differs in having the areæ on the median segment and the nervures all distinctly developed.

Scape of the antennæ black above, yellowish beneath. Head pallid-yellow, suffused with testaceous above ; the occiput, the vertex and front broadly in the middle, black ; the vertex strongly and closely punctured ; the face not quite so strongly ; the front finely punctured in the middle, the sides very smooth and shining ; the mandibles and palpi pallid-yellow ; the tips of the mandibles piceous. Prothorax black, edged above and beneath with pallid-yellow, shining, impunctate. Mesonotum finely punctured, its centre broadly rufo-testaceous, darker in the middle, the sides black ; the scutellum probably testaceous, but the pin goes through it. Median segment with a rounded slope ; its base black ; the areæ all distinctly defined ; the supramedian slightly narrowed towards the base ; truncated at base and apex ; the posterior median area obscu rely transversely striated. Except at the top behind the mesopleuræ, closely punctured ; the upper part to the middle, black ; immediately below the black part, rufous, followed by a pale-yellow band ; the sternum rufous. Metapleuræ black, with a broad rufous mark in the middle on the apical three-fourths, the rufous turning into clear pale-yellow at the apex. Wings hyaline, the stigma and nervures fuscous. Areolet at the top nearly the length of the space bounded by the recurrent and the second transverse cubital nervures ; the recurrent nervure received shortly beyond the middle. Legs fulvous ; the four anterior coxæ for the greater part pallid-yellow. Abdomen rufous, closely punctured ; the basal three-fourths of the petiole black ; its apex closely punctured. Gastrocœli shallow, indistinct, closely punctured.

ICHNEUMON NOVA-ZEALANDICUS, *sp. nov.*

Niger, pedibus abdomineque rufis, capite thoraceque rufo-et flavo-variegatis ; alis hyalinis, nervis stigmateque flavo-testaceis. ♀.   Long. fere 5 mm.

Scape of antennæ rufous, black above, the flagellum absent. Head rufous, the orbits on the inner side and above and beneath on the outer side, as well as the base of the mandibles, yellow ; the front deeply excavated, black ; the vertex blackish, broadly so in the centre ; the face minutely punctured, the vertex aciculated. The mesonotum minutely punctured ; down the centre are two rather broad rufo-testaceous lines, the scutellum and post-scutellum are yellow, suffused with rufous. Median segment sharply oblique, the middle slightly hollowed; the sides broadly rufo-testaceous; there are no keels except the curved lateral ones, and on the apex the testaceous part is bordered on the inner side by a lateral keel. The propleuræ above and beneath bordered with yellow; obscurely striolated; the mesopleuræ black above, bordered with rufous; the middle broadly yellow, the sternum rufous; the base above finely longitudinally striated, the rest punctured; the metapleuræ smooth, shining; a short, wide, deep, oblique furrow at the base above. The coxæ and trochanters are rufous, suffused with yellow. Areolet narrowed at the top, being there not much less in width than the space bounded by the recurrent and the second transverse cubital nervures. Abdomen uniformly ferruginous, shining; the basal three-fourths of the petiole black above; the sheaths of the ovipositor rufous, black at the apex; the ventral surface tinged with yellow.

Comes nearest to *I. utetes,* but that species has the pleuræ and sternum blackish and the mesopleuræ strongly striolated.

DICOELOTUS STRIATIFRONS, *sp. nov.*

Rufus, antennis nigris ; orbitis oculorum, tegulis, linea pronoti, lineis 2 mesonoti scutelloque flavis ; metapleuris striolatis; alis hyalinis, stigmate testaceo. ♀. Long. 6 mm.

Antennæ black; the scape and the basal half of the flagellum brownish beneath; the flagellum almost bare, the scape with a few hairs on the under side. Head shining, the face and clypeus with longish pale hairs; the vertex punctured, except at the sides; the antennal depression closely transversely striated; the front with a shallow longitudinal furrow over the depression ; the clypeus obliquely depressed in the middle at the centre, the depression almost semicircular ; the top with a few punctures ; the centre below the antennæ broadly, roundly and distinctly raised ; the mandibles rufo-testaceous ; the tips black ; the palpi pale-testaceous. The frontal depression black ; the vertex blackish at the ocelli ; the inner orbits narrowly at the bottom, broadly at the top, and narrowly again behind the eyes, yellow. Prothorax in front, the edge of the pronotum, two lines in the centre of the mesonotum, the scutellum except at the apex, the propleuræ and the mesopleuræ over the coxæ, lemon-yellow ; the propleuræ almost entirely black, as is also the sternum ; the upper half of the mesopleuræ, and the metapleuræ, black ; the mesopleuræ strongly punctured, except the usual smooth space behind ; the base above almost longitudinally striated ; the metapleuræ very finely and closely longitudinally striated ; a red and yellow mark over the coxæ. Scutellum flat, large, not much narrowed towards the apex, the post-scutellum rufous, very smooth, and having two large, deep, oval depressions at the base. Median segment shagreened, almost striated in the middle ; the supramedian area longer than broad ; bluntly rounded at the base. The four anterior coxæ coloured like the femora ; the hinder broadly black at the base beneath, and with a yellow mark at the base behind. Abdomen shining, the apex of the fourth, the fifth and the sixth, black. In the fore wings the transverse median nervure is interstitial; the areolet is much narrowed at the top, being there less in length than the space bounded by the recurrent and the second transverse cubital nervures.

Appears to be a true *Dicoelotus*, the first species of the genus recorded, I believe, out of Europe, The foveæ at the base of the post-scutellum are large and deep, more so, in fact, than in most species of the genus.

CRYPTINA.

MESOSTENUS ALBO-PICTUS Sm.

Smith, *Trans. Entom. Soc.*, 1876, p. 477, pl. IV. f. 1.
One ♀. A large and handsome species.

HEMITELES DESTRUCTIVUS, *sp. nov.*

Niger, pedibus abdomineque rufo-testaceis, petiolo nigro ; alis hyalinis, stigmate fusco. ♀. Long. 5 mm. ; terebra 1 mm.

Head absent. Thorax entirely black, shining ; the pro- and meso-thorax thickly covered with short pale hair, almost impunctate, the lower part of the pro- and meso-pleuræ strongly longitudinally striated, except the usual impunctate spot on the apex of the latter ; the part of the metapleuræ below the keel obliquely striated, that above it rugose. The median segment rugosely punctured ; the areæ all distinctly defined ; the sides with a distinct tooth near the top of the apical part Legs rufo-testaceous ; the trochanters paler ; the hinder coxæ black, except at the apex. Wings clear hyaline, the stigma and the nervures paler ; the recurrent nervure is received in the apical third of the cellule, the tegulæ pallid-testaceous. Petiole black, finely and closely longitudinally striated ; apical segments of abdomen thickly covered with short pale hair.

PIMPLIDES.

RHYSSA SEMIPUNCTATA.

The species described by Mr. Kirby (*Trans. Entom. Soc.*, 1883, p. 202) cannot be referred to *Rhyssa*. I am not quite certain to which genus it belongs ; assuredly not to *Rhyssa*, which *inter alia* differs in having the mesonotum transversely striolated.

Compared with *Pimpla* the face is longer, the eyes

being separated from the base of the mandibles; the clypeus is much larger, more elongate and narrowed gradually towards the apex; the mandibles have two teeth at the apex; the eyes are distinctly margined on the inner side; the centre of the mesonotum at the base is separated by deep crenulated furrows into a cone-shaped lobe, the sides of the pronotum being raised at the base of the furrows, which are produced as one a short distance beyond the apex of the lobe; the scutellum is narrowed towards the apex, curved at the base; the keels are large and acute. The median segment is strongly and uniformly transversely striated; the centre flatly raised; the sides stoutly keeled; the keels ending in a stout blunt tooth; the apex with an oblique slope and with the sides keeled. The top and base of the mesopleuræ are depressed; the edges of the depression crenulated; in the middle and reaching near to the apex is a wide, deep, slightly oblique furrow; the hinder edge has a wide, flat, slightly oblique, crenulated furrow; and, in front of this on the lower side, is a short, wide, oblique depression. The legs are stout; the hinder femora have, shortly beyond the middle, a short, somewhat triangular tooth; the tibiæ are spined, especially the hinder, the middle pair having only a few and the anterior none at all; the tarsi are spined; the claws long, curved, simple. The abdomen smooth, shining and impunctate throughout; the base oblique, not hollowed; the sides of the second and third obliquely furrowed, the furrows being more distinctly defined than in *Pimpla*. The fore tarsi are twice the length of the tibiæ; the middle segments of the abdomen broader than long; the ovipositor issues from a ventral cleft.

The ♂ offers no noteworthy generic character wherein it differs from the ♀.

The toothed posterior femora, spined tibiæ, elongated face, deeply lobed mesonotum, furrowed mesopleuræ

and median segment form a combination of dis-
tinctive characters which warrants a new genus being
formed for this species, which I would name *Xenopimpla.*
The ♂ is not described by Kirby.   It agrees generally
in coloration with the ♀; but the scutellar keels, the
apex of the scutellum, the post-scutellum, the edges
of the apex of the mesonotum, and the metanotal spines
are yellow ; the furrow on the mesopleuræ and the apex
of the mesopleuræ, are black, but the extreme apex of
the latter is yellow ; the petiole is bordered with yellow,
the yellow band being narrowed in the middle ; the yellow
marks on the abdomen extend to the fifth segment ; one,
two, or three of the apical segments may be red ; the
hinder tibiæ may be for the greater part blackish and they
are less strongly spined.   In both sexes the quantity of
black on the antennæ varies, as does also the amount of
violaceous colour in the wings.

LISSONOTA TINCTIPENNIS, *sp. nov.*

*Rufa ; antennis nigris ; thorace albo-maculato ; alis
fere flavo-hyalinis.* ♀. Long. 10 mm.

Antennæ entirely black, covered with a microscopic
down ; the scape slightly black-haired. Head shining, the
vertex closely punctured, almost glabrous ; the face
sparsely covered with short white hair ; the orbits all
round, but more narrowly at the top, and the mandibles,
white ; the mandibular teeth blackish ; the mandibles at
their base piceous ; the palpi pale-rufous. Thorax dark-
rufous ; the middle of the mesonotum broadly, the sides
less distinctly, the lower part of the propleuræ, the sides
and top of the mesopleuræ, the hinder part of the mesosternum and the edges of the metathorax, black ; the
base of the pronotum, a somewhat triangular large mark
on either side of the mesonotum at the base, two elongate

marks, dilated at the middle, at its apex, the scutellum, the post-scutellum, a large somewhat oval mark at the base of the mesopleuræ, and a large oblique one on the metapleuræ, white. The median segment transversely aciculated, less strongly so at the base; before the apex is a stout transverse curved keel; and in the centre are a few transverse striæ. Legs entirely rufous; the fore pair slightly paler in tint. Abdomen smooth, shining, impunctate. Wings hyaline, iridescent, and with a slight fuscous tinge; the stigma and nervures fuscous; the areolet oblique.

Allied to *L. flavo-picta* Sm., but that has only two yellow marks on the mesonotum, no yellow on the metapleuræ, and the coxæ are yellow. *L. albo-picta* Sm., has the head black.

TRYPHONIDES.

CHORINÆUS (?) FORTIPES, *sp. nov.*

Long: 5 mm. ♀.

The specimen of this species unfortunately wants the head, but it differs so much from *C. nigripes* that there can be no doubt of their distinctness. It differs from *C. nigripes* in the petiole having two strong keels down its centre, which is, further, much more distinctly raised and separated from the sides.

Pro- and meso-notum shining, closely and strongly punctured, thickly covered with black hair; the scutellum with large distinctly separated punctures. Median segment depressed and distinctly margined at the base, rough, indistinctly punctured, thickly covered with greyish hair; the two keels in the centre much stronger than they are in *C. nigripes*, and are continued round the sides of the apex. All the pleuræ smooth and shining, sparsely haired; the sternum thickly covered with fuscous hair. Wings fusco-hyaline; the stigma and nervures dark-fuscous ; the transverse cubital nervures united at the top ; the recurrent nervure is received in the apical third of the cellule. Legs black, thickly covered with longish white hair ; the base and apex of the anterior tibiæ and the fore tarsi for the greater part testaceous. Abdomen strongly punctured, thickly covered with short pale hair ; the petiole strongly keeled down the centre to shortly beyond the middle ; the base not much depressed in the centre.

The two species I have here referred to *Chorinæus* agree better with that genus than with any other. The keels on the second and third abdominal segments characteristic of *Chorinæus* can hardly be said to exist ; the femora and the legs generally are stouter than they are in *e.g.* the European *C. funebris ;* while both species differ in the areolet being complete.

CHORINÆUS NIGRIPES, *sp. nov.*

Niger, tibiis tarsisque anticis testaceis ; alis fere hyalinis. ♀.

Long. fere 6 mm.

Face at the sides finely and closely transversely striated, in the centre irregularly rugose ; covered with long, soft white hair ; the front and vertex shining, impunctate ; more thickly covered with shorter hair than on the face ; the palpi dark-testaceous. Thorax shining, impunctate ; the pro- and meso-notum thickly covered with short dark hair ; the median segment coarsely shagreened, except in the middle at the apex where it is shining and impunctate ; down the centre are two distinct keels which slightly diverge at the apex. Pleuræ shining, impunctate ; the metapleuræ on the lower side bordered by a stout keel. Legs black ; the front knees, tibiæ and tarsi, testaceous ; the four hinder tarsi of a darker testaceous colour, the metatarsus being almost fuscous. Wings hyaline, very slightly infuscated ; the stigma almost black ;

the nervures testaceous ; the areolet narrow, longish ; the recurrent nervures united at the top ; the first transverse cubital nervure thick, the second narrow, faint on lower side ; the recurrent nervure received near the apex of the areolet and largely bullated at the top; the first transverse cubital nervure bulges out backwards, forming a triangle. The basal three segments of the abdomen strongly punctured, the others impunctate, thickly covered with longish pale hair.

BASSUS GENEROSUS, *sp. nov.*

Niger, orbitis oculorum, ore, palpis, linea pronoti, scutello, tegulis, lineaque tibiarum posticarum albis ; pedibus rufis ; tarsis posticis nigris ; alis hyalinis, stigmate fusco. ♀.

Long. 6 mm.

Head black ; the face punctured, sparsely covered with short fuscous hair ; the mouth, the base of the mandibles, palpi and inner orbits, white ; the mandibular teeth piceous and black.   Thorax black ; a large broad mark on the side of the mesonotum at the base, reaching to the tegulæ, the tegulæ, tubercles, a triangular mark on the pleuræ below the base of the hind wings, the greater part of the scutellum and the post-scutellum, yellowish-white. Median segment closely punctured ; the keels stout ; the supramedian area wider than long ; the large median area rounded on each side at the top ; stoutly transversely striolated. Propleuræ distinctly punctured ; the mesopleuræ almost impunctate, especially in the middle behind ; the metapleuræ minutely punctured. Legs red ; the fore coxæ and the middle at the base, black; the apices of the coxæ and the trochanters yellow ; the base of the hinder tibiæ broadly black ; a broad white band towards the middle ; at the apex of the white band they are black, the apex itself being rufous.   The stigma is for the greater part black ; the base broadly testaceous.

Abdomen black ; the apical half of the second and the basal half of the third rufo-testaceous ; the apex of the second segment yellow ; down the centre of the petiole (but not reaching the apex) are two keels ; the extreme apex smooth, but, in front of this smooth part, there are short, stout, longitudinal keels ; the second segment has, shortly beyond the middle, a wide, deep, transverse furrow, which is finely longitudinally striolated, and, in the middle, is bent a little backwards ; the base of the segment is coarsely but closely punctured ; the third segment has also a transverse furrow.

MESOLEPTUS SYBARITA, *sp. nov.*

Niger, capite thoraceque albo-maculatis, apice metanoti, abdomine pedibusque rufis; alis hyalinis, stigmate fusco. ♂.

Long. 9 mm.

Antennæ black ; the scape reddish in the middle beneath. Head lemon-yellow ; the occiput except at the sides, the vertex except at the orbits, and a broad line down the face to the base of the clypeus, black ; finely punctured, very sparsely covered with short pale hair ; the mandibles lemon-yellow, black at the apex ; the palpi yellow, without a lemon tint. Thorax black; a broad line on the pronotum not reaching to the base, two lines in the centre of the mesonotum extending from the base to the apex, the base of the lines dilated outwardly, club-shaped and touching the pronotum, the scutellum except at the apex, post-scutellum, the prosternum, a large oblique mark on the mesopleuræ, the apex of the propleuræ to near the bottom, the tubercles, a large oblique mark on the apex of the metapleuræ and a small one at the base above, lemon-yellow ; the middle lobes of the mesonotum and the apical half of the metanotum brownish-red : above the yellow mark on the mesopleuræ is a large brownish-red mark ; the upper part of the yellow mark being bordered by the same colour; the reddish apex of the metanotum transversely striated. Legs fulvous, the four anterior coxæ, the trochanters and the upper part of the hinder coxæ, lemon-yellow. Areolet triangular; the nervures blackish, the costa dark-testaceous. Abdomen fulvous-red above; the ventral surface, except at the apex, lemon-yellow.

<h2 style="text-align:center">MESOLEPTUS COMPARATUS, sp. nov.</h2>

Long. 9-10 mm.

Differs from *M. sybarita* in the thorax being almost entirely brownish-red, in the pleuræ having no yellow marks, in the mesonotum having only two small yellow marks, and in the face being broadly black in the middle.

Head black; the orbits of the eyes except for a small space below the top on the outer side, the clypeus, base of mandibles, palpi, two short lines on the apex of the mesonotum, the scutellum, post-scutellum, the pro-thorax broadly beneath, a small obscure mark on the mesopleuræ in the centre, and a large oblique mark in the centre of the metapleuræ, yellow; the middle lobe of the pronotum, the parts at the sides of the scutella, the base of the median segment broadly in the middle, the mark being narrowed towards the apex, the middle of the pro-pleuræ, the top and base of the mesopleuræ broadly, the mesonotum in the middle behind, the edges of the meta-pleuræ at the base and beneath, black. The puncturing on the mesothorax is not very strong; the sides of the scutellum obscurely longitudinally striated. Legs reddish, except a large black mark on the hinder coxæ beneath. Areolet oblique, irregular; the transverse cubital nervures not united at the top. Petiole closely and strongly acicu-lated except at the apex; the second segment aciculated, the others smooth; the three apical broadly blackish.

OPHIONIDES.

OPHION PUNCTATUS, *sp. nov.*

Long. 11 mm.

Head rufous, the inner orbits bright lemon-yellow, the colour becoming paler as it unites with the rufous colour of the rest of the head ; the face coarsely and closely punctured, the clypeus at the base sparsely punctured, its apex almost impunctate ; thickly covered with short pale hair ; the mandibles pale lemon-yellow, the teeth black ; the hinder orbits obscure-yellow ; the palpi pale-yellow. The two basal joints of the antennæ are rufous. Thorax rufous, shining ; the pro- and meso-notum closely and rather strongly punctured, closely covered with a microscopic pile ; the scutellum is not so darkly coloured as the mesonotum, and has the punctures more widely punctured. Median segment finely closely rugose, thickly covered with short fuscous hair. Propleuræ closely and somewhat strongly punctured, thickly covered wlth short fuscous hair ; the base raised and paler in colour. The mesopleuræ strongly punctured ; the metapleuræ with the punctures more widely separated, and smaller at base ; at the base is a smooth, curved, and in front of the spiracles is a wider, deeper, oblique, furrow, which becomes wider towards the apex, and clearly separating the pleuræ into two unequal parts. Wings hyaline, with a fuscous tinge, the nervures and stigma dark-fuscous. Tegulæ lemon-yellow. Abdomen not quite so dark-luteous as the thorax ; the petiole with an elongated depression extending from the front of the spiracles to a slightly greater distance behind them, in the centre on the top ; its apex being slightly wider than the base ; the ventral surface of the second and third segments pallid lemon-yellow. The genital armature coloured like the abdomen.

The only New Zealand species of *Ophion* with

punctured thorax is *Ophion inutilis* Sm., No. 2. *Trans. Entom. Soc.*, 1878, p. 2, but that appears to be a quite different form, *O. inutilis*, No. 2, having the nervures and stigma ferruginous, while in our species the stigma is black, without a tint of reddish colour; no mention being made of any yellow colour in the eyes in *O. inutilis.* I write "*O. inutilis*, No. 2," for Smith actually described in the *Trans. Entom. Soc.*, 1876, p. 478, another *O. inutilis*, which is treated as identical with the 1878 specimen by Kirby (*Trans. Entom. Soc.*, 1881, p. 45). The 1876 specimen has also no yellow on the head, nor is there any mention of the thorax being punctured, as it is said to be in No. 2.

PANISCUS EPHIPPIATUS Sm.

Apparently a common species, if I have correctly identified our species with Smith's, whose description is not clear. He says, "mesothorax black," which would mean the entire mesothorax ; but lower down he says, "sternum black," words which are unnecessary if the whole mesothorax is black. In the Greymouth example only the mesonotum and mesosternum are black ; the orbits are obscure yellow ; the stigma and nervures dark fuscous. The face is closely, the clypeus more widely, punctured ; the tips of the mandibles black ; the ocellar region deep-black ; the outer ocelli bordered by a distinct furrow on the outer side. The black on the mesonotum does not extend to the sides, nor to the edge of the central lobe. The basal half of the propleuræ obliquely striated ; the upper half of the mesopleuræ closely punctured ; the centre at the base rough ; the lower part punctured ; the metapleuræ closely punctured above, the lower part irregularly longitudinally striated ; the scutellum closely punctured, the sides sharply keeled. The median segment coarsely and closely transversely striolated, more strongly towards the apex. Wings hyaline, the nervures and stigma dark-fuscous.

PANISCUS FOVEATUS, *sp. nov.*

Long. 17-18 mm.

A larger species than *P. ephippiatus ;* may be known from it by the absence of black on the vertex and thorax, and by the form of the post-scutellum, which is much more convex, has the sides distinctly keeled, and is deeply depressed at the base, the depression being almost bifurcate, through the centre being raised.

The flagellum of the antennæ infuscated ; the face and clypeus pallid-yellow; the face more closely punctured than the clypeus ; the tips of the mandibles black. Mesonotum shagreened ; the scutellum closely punctured, much narrowed towards the apex ; the post-scutellum rugosely punctured, the sides at the base (bordering the depression) sharply keeled. Median segment coarsely transversely striated, at its base in the centre is a wide, curved, deep furrow as in *P. ephippiatus.* The propleuræ obscurely obliquely striated ; the apex closely punctured ; the mesopleuræ closely, but not strongly, punctured ; the metapleuræ behind the spiracles finely punctured, the rest much more coarsely punctured, on the lower side almost longitudinally striolated, the lower part of the mesopleuræ is not depressed as it is in *P. ephippiatus.* Wings hyaline, the nervures blackish, the stigma fuscous. The abdomen is uniformly luteous, the apex not being darkened ; the sides of the petiole at the base widely excavated.

LIMNERIA ZEALANDICA, *sp. nov.*

Nigra, abdomine rufo, basi late nigro ; pedibus rufis, coxis posticis nigris, trochanteribus flavis ; alis hyalinis, stigmate testaceo. ♀.

Long. 7 ; terebra 2.5 mm.

Antennæ nearly as long as the body, black ; the scape testaceous beneath ; the flagellum thickly covered with short black hair. Head black ; the mandibles yellow ; their teeth piceous-black ; below the antennæ thickly covered with silvery hair ; the vertex more thickly with shorter black hair. Thorax black, hardly shining, except on the apex of the meso- and the base of the meta-pleuræ ; the propleuræ at the apex longitudinally striolated. The median segment with a curved keel near the base ; on the metapleuræ a keel unites to the spiracle, and, from near the apex of this keel, a less distinct one runs to opposite the middle of the coxæ. Legs rufous ; the hind coxæ black ; the four anterior trochanters pale-yellow ; the posterior tarsi infuscated. Petiole black, except the apex, which is very shining and testaceous, at the sides finely striated ; the rest aciculated ; the second segment black ; the apex broadly, the sides narrowly, rufous. The areolet oblique, narrow, the nervures touching at the top ; the areolet projecting beneath ; the recurrent nervure received beyond the middle of it.

BRACONIDÆ.

ASCOGASTER CRENULATUS, *sp. nov.*

Niger, tarsis fuscis ; alis fumatis. ♀. Long. fere 5 mm.

Head almost opaque, except the vertex, which is smooth and shining in the centre, covered, especially in front, with a white pubescence ; the mandibles pale-yellow at the apex ; the teeth piceous ; it is closely punctured, the vertex and front being less strongly punctured than the lower parts. Thorax covered with a microscopic white pile ; the pronotum irregularly longitudinally striolated in front ; the striations in the hollowed middle being the larger. Mesonotum finely and closely punctured ; down the middle are two shallow, striated furrows. Scutellum

with the punctures more distinct and more widely separated
than on the mesonotum ; its base is hollowed and divided
by eight strong keels ; it is narrowed towards the apex ;
its sides are straight, and it forms almost a triangle ; the
mesonotum at its sides is strongly longitudinally striated ;
the striations being widely separated ; on either side at
its apex is a smooth, shining, transverse space.   The
base of the median segment bears short, thick, longitudinal
keels, separated from the rest of the segment by a stout
transverse one, the rest of the segment being reticulated,
bordered on the inner side by a longitudinal keel, the edge
itself being also stoutly keeled.   The propleuræ in front
finely transversely striated ; the centre hollowed, strongly
irregularly and deeply striolated ; the striations on the
apex much weaker ; the mesopleuræ above with shallow,
irregular punctures ; the lower side much more strongly
punctured, almost reticulated ; the metapleuræ strongly
irregularly reticulated.   Legs black ; the extreme apices
of the femora, and the base of the tibiæ testaceous ; the
spurs whitish ; the tibiæ and tarsi closely covered with
silvery pubescence.   The base of the abdomen coarsely,
the apex finely and closely longitudinally striated.   Radial
nervure elongate, reaching to the end of the wing, being
nearly as long as the cubital ; the second transverse cubital
nervure is very faint.

METEORUS NOVA-ZEALANDICUS, sp. nov.

Rufus, capite pedibusque pallide flavis, alis hyalinis,
stigmate flavo, basi fusco. ♀.

Long. 5.5 ; terebra 2 mm.

Head shining ; the face covered with white hair, the
vertex more thickly with shorter fuscous hair ; the teeth of
the mandibles black, piceous at the base ; the front finely
transversely striated ; below the antennæ are a few short
longitudinal striæ.   Thorax uniformly rufous in colour ;

finely and closely rugosely punctured ; the apex of the median segment covered with moderately long, white hair, the base with shorter fuscous hair. The propleuræ irregularly horizontally striolated at the base; the upper part being almost entirely black; the mesopleuræ at the top (especially at the base) strongly irregularly striolated and reticulated; the lower part is widely hollowed, the hollow being strongly and somewhat obliquely striolated. Median segment strongly and closely rugosely punctured ; the base in the middle ĵwith 2 or 3 short longitudinal keels ; the metapleuræ near the top with a stout curved keel, beneath which at the base it is horizontally striated ; the mesopleuræ at the apex raised, almost carinate, the keel being smooth and shining at the top. Legs pallid-yellow ; the hind coxæ and apex of the hind femora rufous ; the hinder tibiæ and tarsi not so pale in colour. Wings hyaline with a faint fuscous hue ; the nervures pallid-fuscous ; the stigma pale-yellow, darker at the base. Petiole rufous ; finely and closely punctured ; the base darker, almost transversely striated ; the rest of the abdomen lighter in colour, especially towards the apex ; the second segment is finely punctured ; the others very smooth.

The first abdominal segment has " tracheal grooves " and is dilated in the middle.   It is longer and more slender than usual.   The second cubital cellule is slightly narrowed at the top.   The antennæ unfortunately have been lost. The radial areolet of the hind wings is not geminated by a transverse nervure.

ALYSIA STRAMINEIPES, *sp. nov.*

Nigra, pedibus flavis ; alis hyalinis, stigmate nigro. ♀.
Long. 4 mm.

Antennæ black ; the scape testaceous ; the flagellum covered closely with a microscopic pile ; the joints not clearly separated, the third longer than the fourth. Head shining ; the face closely, the front and vertex sparsely, covered with short, black hair. Pro- and meso-thorax shining, closely punctured ; the median segment coarsely rugosely punctured, sparsely covered with longish black hairs ; the metapleuræ rugosely punctured at the sides, the middle with wide, deep, widely separated punctures. The hinder edge of the mesopleuræ crenulated ; its base distinctly punctured, the punctures clearly separated, but not by a great distance from each other ; the upper part with the punctures closer, smaller and shallower ; on the lower side, but not touching the base, is a wide, deep, curved furrow, indistinctly crenulated in the middle. The upper part of the propleuræ stoutly striated ; the upper two striæ stout ; on the lower side immediately over the coxæ are two much stouter keels. Median segment coarsely rugosely reticulated. Legs entirely fulvous-yellow ; the femora sparsely, the tibiæ and tarsi thickly, covered with white hair. Wings hyaline ; the stigma large, blackish ; the costa and nervures paler ; the first abscissa of the radius very short, not one-half the length of the space between the recurrent and the first transverse cubital nervure. The petiole above closely, its apex more sparsely and not so strongly, punctured ; the rest of the abdomen very smooth and shining ; the apices of the segments pallid-yellow.

The only specimen is not in good condition, but I believe I have described correctly its salient specific points. It appears to be an *Alysia* as defined by Foerster in his generic synopsis of the family. (*Verh. Ver. Rheinl.* XIX. p. 263.)

EVANIIDÆ.

GASTERUPTION PEDUNCULATUM Schl.

Foenus unguiculatus Smith, *Trans. Entom. Soc.,* 1869 p. 480, pl. IV., f. 8.

Gasteruption pedunculatum Schletterer, *Ann. K. K. Natur. Hofmus. Wien*, 1890, p. 467.

One ♂ and one ♀.

In both examples the pronotum is rufous, except in the middle, the rufous colour being narrowest at the top; the mesopleuræ are broadly rufous immediately over the sternum; there is a curved rufous band over the hinder coxæ, and a narrower oblique one immediately in the middle above it. The amount of red on the legs varies. In the ♂ the amount of white pubescence on the prothorax is much greater than it is in the ♀, unless it be that it has been rubbed off from the latter in my specimens.

PROCTOTRUPIDÆ.

PROCTOTRUPES MACULIPENNIS Cam.

Cameron, *Manchester Memoirs*, 1888, p. 175.
One specimen.

MALVINA PUNCTATA Cam.

Manchester Memoirs, 1889, p. 13.
Four examples.

BETYLA FULVA Cam.

Manchester Memoirs, 1889, p. 13.

This species was described by the Rev. T. A. Marshall in the *Entom. Mon. Mag.*, November 1892, under the name of *Tanyzonus bolitophilæ*, which name must give place to my earlier one.

Mr. Marshall describes both sexes. The ♂ is winged, and has the thorax fully developed, not narrow and contracted as in the wingless ♀, which has 15-jointed antennæ, while the ♂ has them 14-jointed, much thinner, attenuated towards the apex, and with the third joint emarginate.

Mr. G. V. Hudson discovered the species at Wellington, New Zealand, to be a parasite on the luminous "Glow Worm" *Bolitophila luminosa.* *Bolitophila* is a species of Diptera.

FORMICIDÆ.

MONOMORIUM NITIDUM Sm.

Described by Smith as a *Tetramorium.* Common at Greymouth; and, according to Forel, at Mount Cook, on the Island of Timaru, at an elevation of 2,540 feet.

HUBERTIA STRIATA Sm.

This was also erroneously referred to *Tetramorium.* It is more related to *Monomorium;* and a new genus, *Hubertia*, has been formed for its reception by Forel, *C.R. Soc. Entom. Belgique*, 1890. Found at Greymouth and at Mount Cook along with *M. nitidum.*

For an interesting description of the habits of the above-mentioned ants, as observed at Ashburton, the reader is referred to a paper "On the origin of Ants' Nests," by Mr. W. W. Smith in *Entom. Mon. Mag.*, March, 1892, pp. 60-65.* The nests are formed under stones partly buried in the sandy soil, on the terraces of the river and in stony places on the plains.

In the nests of the ants are found sundry inquilines. There are two species of Homoptera a species of *Ripersia* and *Dactylopius poæ* Maskell, both feeding on the roots of the grasses among which the ants' nests are placed; a beetle, *Diarthrocera formicæphiia* Brown, an isopod, *Platyarthrus*, and some mites. It is noteworthy that the coccid genus, *Ripersia*, and the crustacean, *Platyarthrus*, are found inhabiting ants' nests in Europe.

PONERA CASTANEA Sm.

Several examples.

* For a description of a great flight of *M. nitidum*, see W. W. Smith, *Entom. Mon. Mag.*, 1890, p. 321.

APHAENOGASTER ANTARCTICUS Sm.
Two females.

FOSSORES.

CRABRO (RHOPALUM) JOCOSUS, *sp. nov.*

Long. 8-9 mm.

Comes near to *C. perforator* Sm. ; differs in having less yellow on the legs and none on the mesonotum.

Head black ; the cheeks and clypeus densely covered with silvery pubescence ; the front and vertex alutaceous, sparsely covered with microscopic down ; the ocelli ·.· ; the vertex depressed in the centre, where there is a furrow running down from the ocelli ; close to the eyes on the inner side, nearly opposite the lower ocellus, is a short, moderately deep, curved depression. Antennæ black ; the basal joints of the flagellum testaceous beneath ; the third joint slightly, the fourth largely, produced beneath ; the sixth deeply incised at the base, the apex largely dilated ; the fifth joint ovate. The mandibles piceous before the teeth ; there is one large apical and a shorter basal tooth. Pronotum at the middle distinctly separated from the mesothorax ; in the centre above broadly hollowed, the sides behind depressed, the middle raised, rounded ; the edge of the pronotum near the tegulæ white. Mesonotum and scutellum shining, impunctate, glabrous ; a deep, large, oval depression at the side of the post-scutellum. Down the centre of the median segment is a deep, moderately wide furrow. At the base of the mesopleuræ an oblique, wide, crenulated furrow ; in the centre above a small round depression ; the metapleuræ are broadly depressed at the base. Legs black ; the base of the fore femora, the fore tibiæ except a black line behind, the fore tarsi, the apex of the middle femora, the middle tibiæ except behind, the middle tarsi except the apical joint and the second and third joints of the hinder tarsi, yellow.   Wings hyaline; the stigma and nervures black.   Abdomen shining; the apical segments covered with short pale hair; the pygidium opaque, covered with longish white hair.

TARANGA.

Under this name Mr. W. F. Kirby (*Trans. Entom. Soc.* 1883, p. 201, fig.) describes a genus *Taranga* "apparently allied to *Pemphredon*" but which is really related to *Pison.* Kohl (*Ann. K. K. Natur. Hofmus. Wien*, XI. p. 458) regards it as a division of *Pison.* Bingham (*Fauna of India, Hym.* i. p. 218) says that he has "taken specimens of *Pison* with three cubital cells in one fore wing, only two in the other.   Such seems to be the case with the allied genus *Taranga* Kirby.   Kohl unites *Taranga* to *Pison*; but from a careful examination of the type, I have come to the conclusion that they are distinct." I have noticed myself that the outer nervure of the pendicular cellule tends to become obliterated in species where it is normally present.   The neuration in *Taranga* appears to be normal, and not merely an individual aberration ; but still I cannot regard it in any other light than as a division of *Pison.* Otherwise the species with neuration differing from the type, *e.g., Pisonites*, would also have to be treated as distinct genera.

PISON PRUINOSUS, *sp. nov.*

Niger, opacus, capite thoraceque longe albo-hirtis; alis fere hyalinis. ♀.   Long. 16 mm.

Antennæ opaque, the scape and basal joints of the flagellum thickly covered with longish pale hair.   Head covered thickly with long greyish hair, which is thicker and more silvery below the eye incision.   Apex of clypeus rounded in the middle.   Mandibles shining, the base with long silvery hair. Thorax opaque, alutaceous, thickly covered with longish white hair, longest and thickest on the scutellum and median segment. Apex of the median segment with with an oblique slope ; the basal half in the centre with a wide, moderately deep furrow, from which run some curved, oblique keels ; the base of the slope coarsely punctured ; the rest with strong, transverse, distinctly separated striations. Pleuræ and sternum with small, shallow, distinctly separated punctures ; the sternum depressed in the centre, down which runs a straight, stout keel. Coxæ, trochanters and femora covered somewhat thickly with longish white hair ; the tibiæ and tarsi pruinose. Wings fusco-hyaline ; the extreme apex smoky ; the second cubital cellule triangular ; in length scarcely half the length of the pedicle ; the first recurrent nervure received shortly, but distinctly, in front of the cubital ; the second interstitial ; the second transverse cubital nervure near the top, and both branches at the bottom are bullated. Abdomen opaque, the segments at the apices banded with silvery pubescence ; the basal two ventral segments sparsely covered with white hair ; the apical more thickly with longer fuscous hair ; the base of the second segment is smooth, raised, and, in the middle, projects into a somewhat triangular area.

P. morosus Sm., is a smaller species than this, has the head, thorax and abdomen more shining, and much less pilose ; the furrows on the median segment shorter and shallower ; its head is more developed behind ; the abdomen deeply excavated in the middle at the base ; the depression on the mesopleuræ wider and deeper ; the pedicle of the second cubital cellule hardly longer than the appendicular cellule ; the second transverse cubital nervure is more rounded and curved at the bottom ; the second cubital cellule at the top is hardly so long as the second at the bottom, while in *P. morosus* it is longer ;

the transverse nervure is received distinctly in front of the transverse basal; in *P. pruinosus* it is interstitial. *P. tuberculatus* Sm. differs in being much smaller—only 3 lines—and in having two minute tubercles on the second, third and fourth ventral segments near their apical margin.

PISON MOROSUS Sm.

One specimen.

GORYTES CARBONARIUS Sm.

An example of this, apparently common, species has the second transverse cubital nervure completely obliterated. *Gorytes trichiosoma* Cam. is probably only a form of *G. carbonarius.*

TACHYTES DEPRESSUS Sauss.

Reise der Novara, Hymen. p. 69.
Three specimens.

TACHYTES SERICOPS Sm.

One example.

TACHYTES HELMSI Cam.

Manchester Memoirs, 1888, p. 182.
One example.

POMPILIDÆ.

The *Pompilidæ* appear to be the commonest, largest and most handsome of the New Zealand Hymenoptera. Under the name of *Sphex* one of the species has been recorded by Mr. Potts (probably *S. Wakefieldi*), as preying on spiders, with which the *Pompilidæ* provision their nests. Mr. Potts (*Nature*, XXX. p. 267) says : "A species of *Sphex* [read *Salius*] with orange-coloured body deposits the benumbed or torpid bodies of spiders in some crevice for future use. An individual of this species had its hole in a dry corner beneath the plate of a long veranda. One day I observed it dragging a victim along a gravelled walk that was parallel to the veranda ; the small stones and grit made its progress very difficult. After very trying struggles with these impediments it displayed a remarkable degree of intelligence, by which it gained its ends. It altered its course and made for the veranda, ascending the smooth, painted board that adjoined the gravelled walk. After slowly traversing seven inches of perpendicular, it came to a rounded beading which projected outwards. Now came its supreme moment of physical exertion. The body of the spider apparently was too heavy to render the aid of wings available. After several pauses in its progress it slowly, yet surely, surmounted the difficulty presented by the projecting beading, gained the level boards of the veranda, along which it travelled rapidly with its burden, which it sometimes dragged, sometimes pushed before it. By the expenditure of great exertion in surmounting the beading it gained a smooth and level run to its home of thirty-nine feet."

In Mr. Kirby's Catalogue all the species are described under the name of *Priocnemis*, which name, however, must give place to *Salius*.

a. Fulvous species.

Salius wakefieldi Kirby.

This is by far the commonest of the *Pompilidæ*. In a fresh state the head and thorax are thickly covered with golden pubescence ; but with age this gets abraded, the parts then appearing quite bare and shining.

Salius marginatus Sm.

A much rarer species than *S. Wakefieldi*, to which it has a great resemblance when the latter has the head and

thorax freshly covered with hair. In *S. marginatus,*
however, the head and thorax are quite black, instead of
brownish or mahogany-coloured, the base of the antennæ
black instead of red, while the first and second transverse
cubital nervures are curved, in *S. Wakefieldi* straight
and oblique.

Under the name of *Agenia brouni,* Signor Gribodo
(*Bull. Soc. Entom. Ital.* XVI., 1884) describes a species from
Howich, which agrees closely in coloration, &c., with
S. Wakefieldi, but the latter is a *Salius* not an *Agenia.*

SALIUS FUGAX Fab. (*maculipennis* Sm.).

This is a rare species, and may be known from the
others by its smaller size and by having a stigmal as well
as an apical fuscous cloud in the wings.

b. Black species.

SALIUS MONACHUS *White* (see *Smith*).

One example of this large species.

SALIUS TRIANGULARIS, *sp. nov.*

Long. 10 mm.

Agrees with *S. monachus* Sm. in being entirely black
and in having the head and thorax covered with long
black hair, but is not half its size ; and otherwise may be
readily known from it by the basal abdominal segment
being triangular as seen from the side, the centre being
sharp, the base and apex falling obliquely, whereas in *S.
monachus* the middle is broadly rounded and not sharply
differentiated.

Scape of antennæ densely covered with black hair ;
the second and third joints bare ; the rest missing. The
head covered all over with long black hair, shining ; the
apex of the mandibles rufous ; the hinder ocelli separated
from each other by half the distance they are from the
eyes. Thorax covered with longish black hairs ; the pro-

and meso-thorax shining ; the median segment rounded at the base, the rest oblique ; the apex obscurely transversely striated. The femora sparsely covered with longish black hair. Wings with a shining, fuscous tinge ; the apex of the radial nervure curved ; the second cubital cellule at top and bottom not much more than half the length of the third ; the first transverse cubital nervure sharply, the second slightly, oblique ; the third roundly elbowed at the middle ; the first recurrent nervure received in, the second shortly before, the middle of the cellule. Abdomen shining, impunctate ; the basal slope of the petiole covered with longish black hair ; the apical more thickly with stouter hair ; the apical segment thickly covered with long, stiff, black hair; the hypopygium with the sides broadly rounded; the centre roundly incised.

In certain lights, the wings have a bright, metallic, bronzy iridescence.

SALIUS CARBONARIUS Sm.

Two examples.

SALIUS NITIDIVENTRIS Sm.

A ♂ and ♀.

This is a much smaller species than *S. carbonarius*, and agrees with it in having the body entirely black, shining and almost bare ; but may be known from it by having the apex of the cubital nervure curved instead of straight and by the second cubital cellule at the top being distinctly shorter than the third, while in the other species it is equal in length to it.

AGENIA HUTTONI, *sp. nov.*

Nigra, nitida, albo-pruinosa, alis hyalinis, nervis nigris. ♂. Long. 5 mm.

Head, except on the vertex, thickly covered with

silvery pubescence; the eyes very slightly converging beneath, straight; the hinder ocelli separated from each other by a somewhat less distance than they are from the eyes. The three basal joints of the antennæ black, closely covered with white pubescence. Thorax almost shining, thickly covered with short white pubescence; the median segment elongate, rounded. Legs pruinose. Wings as long as the body; the apex of the radial nervure with a slight curve; the second and third cubital cellules at the top as long as the third; the first transverse cubital nervure at the bottom slightly curved, the rest oblique; the first recurrent nervure is received shortly beyond, the second shortly before, the middle of the cellules. Legs entirely black; the femora sparsely covered with white hair; the tibiæ and tarsi with white pubescence, the apex of the hind tibiæ on the inner side with fulvous pubescence. Abdomen shining, impunctate, the apex with short white hair; the hypopygium large, broadly keeled at the base in the middle; the apex rounded, sparsely covered with long white hair.

ANTHOPHILA.

ANDRENIDÆ.

DASYCOLLETES VESTITUS Sm.

Trans. Entom. Soc., 1876, p. 485.
Two specimens.

DASYCOLLETES HIRTIPES Sm.

Trans. Entom. Soc., 1878, p. 7.
One specimen.

PROSOPIS AGILIS Sm.

Trans. Entom. Soc., 1876, p. 484.
One specimen.

PROSOPIS SULCIFRONS, *sp. nov.*

Nigra, nitida, alis fusco-violaceis. ♀. Long. 8-9 mm.

Head shining, the vertex sparsely covered with long blackish, the face more thickly with short white hair ; the face with shallow punctures, the vertex at the sides much more distinctly punctured ; the centre at and below the ocellar region opaque, alutaceous ; the front between the antennæ carinate. On the inside, at the top of the eyes is a deep distinct longitudinal suture. The clypeus at the apex roundly, but not deeply, curved. Mandibles entirely black, deeply and widely furrowed on the outer side ; the base alutaceous, the apex shining ; the teeth blunt. A curved, shallow, narrow furrow runs down from the antennæ to the bottom of the eyes, bordering the yellow mark ; and, in the centre below the antennæ and joining the lateral ones, is a transverse straight one. The flagellum of the antennæ obscure-brownish on the under side towards the apex ; closely covered with a pale down ; the scape punctured, scarcely dilated towards the apex. On the pronotum is a yellow line, narrowed and almost interrupted in the middle, dilated on the outer side ; the tubercles yellow, the latter having at their apex a thick mass of pale hair. Mesonotum distinctly, but not deeply, punctured ; there is a central and a lateral narrow, not very distinct, furrow, reaching from the base to the middle. Scutellum punctured like the mesonotum, indistinctly keeled down the middle. Median segment alutaceous, its apex oblique, thickly covered with long white hair. Pro-pleuræ sparsely covered with long white hair ; the meso-pleuræ bearing all over shallow punctures ; the furrow distinctly crenulated. The central furrow on the median segment, deep, narrow. Legs entirely black, except the spurs which are pale ; the tibiæ and tarsi thickly covered with silvery hair, the tibiæ especially towards the apex, the femora sparsely covered with soft pale hair; the spurs pale. Wings fuscous, with a violaceous tinge ; the stigma and nervures blackish, the former fuscous on the lower side ; the second cubital cellule narrowed at the top, being there less in length than the space bounded by the recurrent nervures ; the first recurrent nervure is interstitial ; the second distinctly separated from the second transverse cubital. Abdomen shining, impunctuate ; the apex thickly covered with long black hair. The propleuræ at the base are finely indistinctly obliquely striated.

Comes near to *P. laevigata ;* but the description given of its metathorax "smooth", the apex of the abdomen with only " a few black hairs," while in the present species it is thickly covered with long black hairs, does not fit the species here described.

PROSOPIS INNOCENS, *sp. nov.*

Long. 7 mm. ♂ .

Comes near to *P. agilis* Sm., but differs in the shorter second cubical cellule, in the recurrent nervures being completely interstitial, in the pronotum being without any yellow, and the tubercles black, not yellow.

Head dull, not shining, the front and vertex obscurely punctured ; the clypeus, except the apical margin, yellow, the yellow being produced above it as a wedge-shaped mark, which reaches nearly to the enclosed space below the antennæ, its top being irregular, having one side higher than the other. The inner orbits have a yellow line reaching from near the base of the antennæ, where it is narrow, becoming gradually dilated, rounded, narrowing again to thc bottom, but not so narrowly as at the top. The mandibles black on the lower edge, the upper part yellow ; the teeth piccous and black. Antennæ stout, black ; the basal joints of the flagellum brownish beneath ;

the scape curved, only very slightly dilated towards the apex, and obscurely punctured, the lower part fringed with longish pale hairs. Thorax alutaceous, sparsely covered with pale hairs ; the mesonotum and mesopleuræ obscurely punctured ; the base of the mesopleuræ crenulated ; a deep, wide, curved furrow in front of the middle coxæ. On the mesonotum opposite the tegulæ is a curved, shallow furrow. The middle of the median segment has a wide shallow furrow, and bears long pale hair. Legs black, the anterior tibiæ yellow in front ; the apices of the anterior tarsal joints testaceous ; the tibial spurs pale; the tarsi thickly covered, especially at the base, with pale fulvous hair. Wings hyaline, the stigma black, fuscous on the lower side ; the nervures blackish ; the first transverse cubical nervure oblique ; the second obliquely bent towards it (but not sharply) at the top ; the top of the cellule three-fourths of the length of the bottom ; the first recurrent nervure almost, the second completely, interstitial, Abdomen dull, the apices of the segment dull-piceous ; the apical segments fringed with longish hair.

Abstract of the Greymouth Hymenoptera :—

ICHNEUMONIDES	20	⎫
CRYPTIDES	2	⎪
PIMPLIDES	2	⎬ ICHNEUMONIDÆ
TRYPHONIDES ...	5	⎪
OPHIONIDES ...	4	⎭
BRACONIDÆ ...	3	
EVANIIDÆ ...	ɪ	
PROCTOTRUPIDÆ ...	3	
FORMICIDÆ ...	4	
CRABRONIDÆ	ɪ	
LARRIDÆ ...	6	
POMPILIDÆ ...	8	
ANDRENIDÆ	5	
TOTAL ...	64 SPECIES.	

www.ingramcontent.com/pod-product-compliance
Lightning Source LLC
Chambersburg PA
CBHW021642270326
41931CB00008B/1121